MEN CAN BE DICKS

A PARABLE
written & illustrated by Kichi

"MEN CAN BE DICKS"

A Parable

Dedicated to all of us
who love men ....
   and to those men who
   love themselves too much

Written and Illustrated by Kichi

©2019 by JAKichi

OTHER TITLES BY J.A.KICHI:

THE NAKED CENTURION
2776
HOW I SPENT MY AFTERLIFE
EROTOPATHIC
THE SECOND COMING CONSPIRACY
A BRIEF EVOLUTION OF RELIGION
FOOTBALLL IS SOOOOOO GAY
HARD AND HARDER
HARD TIMES
SARAH BELLUM
PRESIDENT OF THE DAMNED
THE DEATH OF A CAT
CIVIL UNREST
HOW TO POUND SOME SENSE INTO A RELIGIOUS NUT JOB
THE REPUBLICAN'TS
TRUMP: A RECIPE FOR FASCISM

"Nobility is being superior to your former self"

— Winston Churchill

Author's Preface

This book is written for the love of men. It is meant to serve as something of a mirror in which all men will see a measure of themselves. And I hope its central parable will help men - and those who love them, male and female – to better understand the dynamics of toxic masculinity. To paraphrase Cassius and Shakespeare, "the fault lies in our stars <u>and</u> in ourselves."

Foreward

Men are beautiful creatures. As a group, as an idea, as physical beings, I love them.

I have been lucky enough to have known mostly good men, Gay and Straight. Men who are in control of their emotions and their power. Men who are sensitive and appealing. Men who share more than they take. My partner is such a man, and he is the best man I have ever known.

But many others who love men, both male and female, have not been quite as lucky as I have been.

It is impossible to avoid the truth that many men act out in ways that damage their wives and partners, damage their own lives and the social fabric. Just read the headlines or the police blotter in any newspaper.

Yes, women can also behave badly, but when a man misbehaves, it can be devastating. That's because men – muscular and powerful - are still in charge mostly everywhere. Men dominate government, business and men dominate the bedroom despite movements for female equality,

Scholars have attributed male aggression to the "Male Warrior Theory," i.e., that men are evolutionarily-predisposed to hunt and kill for food, and presumably, to regard other humans as just another competing male to kill, or a woman to conquer.

Moreover, psychologists have enumerated social-religious factors which can stifle the development of boys to men, tending to frustrate the male biological imperative, limiting a youth's carnal choices and playing havoc with his sexual maturation.

But none of these arguments should be used by any man as an alibi. The human male has a brain and needs to use it, too.

If the image of masculinity is to improve, men must be aware that problems exist. We men need to look in the mirror and recognize who we are and begin to create our individual destinies. The purpose of this book to be one of those mirrors.

"MEN CAN BE DICKS"

A Parable

SAY HELLO TO BILL......

IN ONE IMPORTANT WAY
BILL IS LIKE **ALL** MEN .....

...BILL HAS A PENIS ....

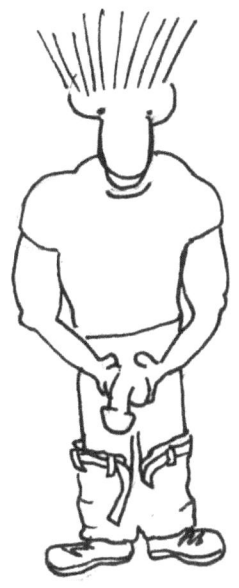

2

AND BILL **LOVES** HIS PENIS ....

ALL MEN DO!

BILL ONCE WROTE
A POEM TO HIS PENIS ....

4

BILL LOVES EVERYTHING ABOUT HIS PENIS

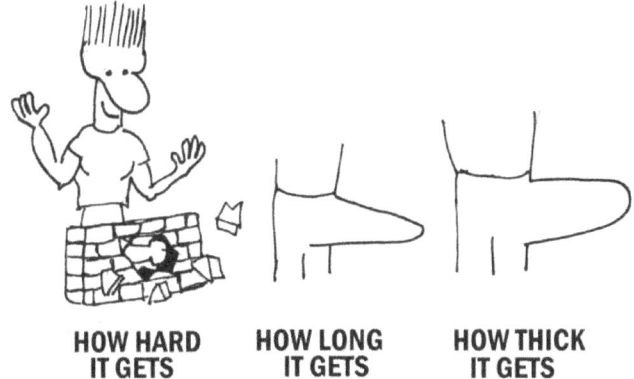

HOW HARD
IT GETS

HOW LONG
IT GETS

HOW THICK
IT GETS

HOW HARD
LONG & THICK
IT GETS
EVEN WHEN
IT SHOULDN'T

6

BILL **LOVES** HIS PENIS MORE THAN ....

HIS MOTHER

HIS WIFE & KIDS

GOD & COUNTRY

FOOTBALL

7

BILL'S PENIS IS ALWAYS CALLING OUT TO HIM:

"Touch Me ......

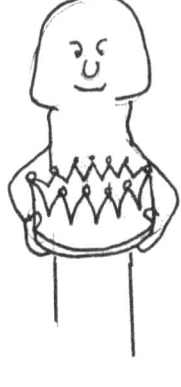

I'LL
MAKE YOU
FEEL LIKE
YOU'RE
KING
OF
THE
WORLD"

BILL'S PENIS
PROVIDES HIM

THE GREATEST
PHYSICAL PLEASURE
KNOWN TO MANKIND!

(NOT COUNTING THE ILLEGAL STUFF)

9

BUT WE CAN'T BLAME BILL ENTIRELY FOR HIS OBSESSION

MOTHER NATURE MADE SURE THAT BILL WOULD BE REMINDED MANY TIMES A DAY THAT HIS PENIS EXISTS ....

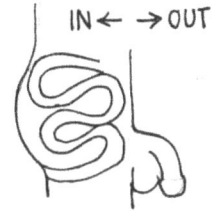

IT'S ON THE OUTSIDE OF HIS BODY

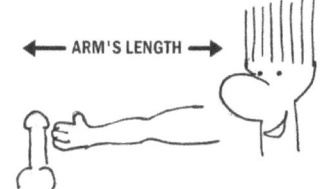

IT'S JUST AN ARM'S LENGTH AWAY

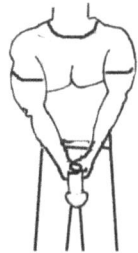

BILL HAS TO PULL IT OUT TO PEE 6 TO 8 TIMES A DAY

AND IT'S JUST **IMPOSSIBLE**
FOR BILL TO FORGET ABOUT
HIS PENIS ....

HE'S ALSO THINKING ABOUT IT WHEN ...

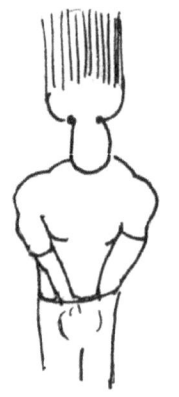

**HIS
BALLS ITCH
(WHICH IS
ALL DAY LONG)**

**HIS PENIS
GETS HARD
INVOLUNTARILY
(WHICH IS
ALL DAY LONG)**

**IS IT ANY WONDER
THAT BILL CAN'T STOP
THINKING ABOUT**

**AND TOUCHING
HIS PENIS
 HUNDREDS OF TIMES
EVERY DAY?!**

12

AND SOMETHING IMPORTANT
TO REMEMBER FOR LATER......

NATURE MADE IT **VERY** EASY
FOR BILL TO USE HIS PENIS

**IT GETS HARD
JUST THINKING
ABOUT GETTING
HARD**

**IT CAN BE
STIMULATED
BY HAND**

**WILLING
RECEPTACLES
NUMBER IN THE
BILLIONS**

BILL SO LOVES HIS PENIS THAT EVEN ON HIS DEATHBED IT WILL BE HIS ONE TRUE LOVE*

*(ALL OF US WHO LOVE A MAN NEED TO REMEMBER THIS)

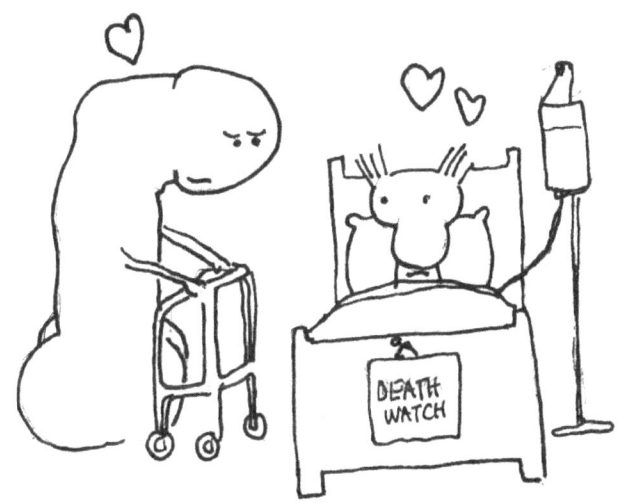

TRIVIA QUESTION

Q: HOW MANY MEN HAVE SAID THEY DON'T WANT TO LIVE WITHOUT A PENIS?

A: EVERY FUCKING MAN ON EARTH

14

BILL
REALLY
REALLY
LOVES HIS PENIS

HIS LOVE
IS UNDYING

15

**BILL LOVES HIS PENIS
SO VERY VERY MUCH**

**AND IT GIVES HIM
(AND HE BELIEVES, OTHERS)
SO MUCH PLEASURE ....**

**THAT HE'S CERTAIN THE WORLD
WILL BEAT A PATH TO HIS DOOR**

16

YOUNG BILL WANTS EVERYONE TO HELP HIM LOVE HIS PENIS

IT IS, AFTER ALL, A MARVEL OF NATURE
AND HE'S BORED WITH WHACKING-OFF

AND THERE WAS LITTLE DISSUADING BILL THAT HIS PENIS WOULD BE POPULAR

BILL FOUND THERE WAS NO SHORTAGE OF PUBESCENT MALE TEAMMATES AND CLASSMATES WHO'D GLADLY WORSHIP HIS BEAUTIFUL PENIS WITH THEIR HAND OR MOUTH OR ANUS

THAT WAS PARTLY DUE TO A BUILD-UP OF EXCESS HORMONES & SPERM

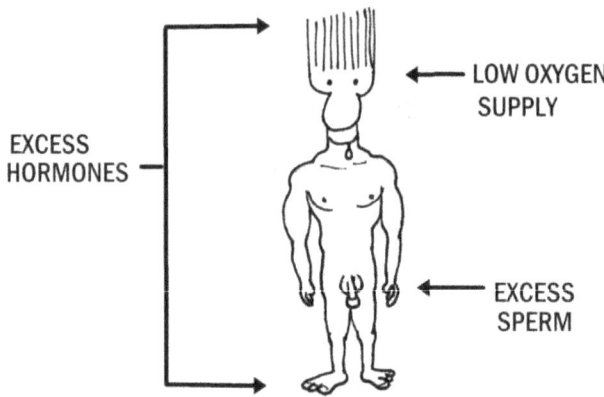

...AND ....
REDUCED BLOOD FLOW TO THE BRAIN FROM MASTURBATION WHICH CAUSED LIGHT-HEADEDNESS AND WHICH STIMULATED AROUSAL EVEN MORE

...AND ....
SOMETHING MORE .....

19

THE POPULARITY OF BILL'S PENIS WAS ALSO ATTRIBUTABLE TO SOCIALIZATION NOT HAVING YET DESTROYED THE
PANSEXUALITY
WE ARE ALL BORN WITH

IN BILL'S EARLY, FORMATIVE YEARS, SOCIETAL NORMS AND CONSTRAINTS

WERE NOT FULLY UNDERSTOOD AND CERTAINLY NOT RESPECTED

IN SCHOOL,
MANY BOYS HAD **NO**
SERIOUS ADVERSION TO **BILL'S**
PENIS AND TO MAKING IT
AND HIM VERY HAPPY

AND BETWEEN THESE BOYS
AND WHACKING OFF

BILL
WAS
VERY
VERY
VERY
HAPPY

23

BUT EVENTUALLY, PRESSURE FROM CHURCH, STATE, FAMILY AND FRIENDS

SCARED MOST* YOUNG MEN STRAIGHT INTO FULFILLING THE EXPECTATIONS OF HETEROSEXUAL SOCIETY

* INCLUDING BILL

24

THE TRANSITIONING TO EXCLUSIVE HETEROSEXUALITY HAS BEEN GOING ON EVER SINCE TRIBES NEEDED BABIES TO GROW INTO WARRIORS

GROWL!

THESE STRICTLY HETEROSEXUAL MEN BECAME A HOT COMMODITY AND USED THEIR MARKETABILITY TO DOMINATE CHURCH, STATE AND MANY FEMALE HEARTS

(Today, such men are called "Alpha Males" or "assholes")

25

AND SOMETHING SIMILAR HAPPENED TO HOMOSEXUAL
SOCIETY AS THOSE PREDISPOSED TO BEING EXCLUSIVELY
& IMMUTABLY GAY GAINED CONTROL OF POWER CENTERS
DICTATING BODY IMAGE, ETHICS, FASHION AND POLITICS

.... **BUT** ....
THAT'S ANOTHER BOOK

26

IN VERY SHORT ORDER, BILL & MOST* OF HIS CLASSMATES WERE SCURRYING TO GIRLS FOR PENIS WORSHIP

* A large majority of those who "moved on" were men who were open to both male/female sexual encounters, but also being persuaded by straight society. A large minority of Bill's peers, those who were immutably gay, didn't have any reason to move on. And as I've said, that another book for another day.

BILL AND HIS CHUMS HAD NO PROBLEM SWITCHING GEARS ...

THEY SWITCHED FROM PECS TO BOOBS, FROM ANUS TO VAGINA WITHOUT MISSING A BEAT

STRAIGHT SOCIETY HAD ASSURED THEM THAT THERE WERE MILLIONS OF WOMEN AS INTERESTED IN THEIR PENISES AS THEY WERE

BUT

AS BILL MADE THE SWITCH, HE BEGAN TO UNDERSTAND THAT GIRLS HAD A DIFFERENT "APPROACH" TO MAKING HIS PENIS HAPPY

29

AS A YOUNGER MAN, BILL HAD
SOME SUCCESS WITH GIRLS
WHO LIKED HIS PENIS ALMOST
AS MUCH AS HE DID ...
MAYBE MORE

BUT
BIOLOGICAL AND SEXUAL
MATURITY BROUGHT CHANGE ...

AS HE ENTERED **THE ADULT** WORLD,
BILL DISCOVERED THAT WHILE WOMEN
MIGHT LIKE THE IDEA OF PENIS WORSHIP,
GETTING THEM TO DO IT LICKETY-SPLIT LIKE
A HORNY YOUNG GUY WASN'T SO EASY

BILL WAS ANGRY ....
BILL WAS CONFUSED

SOCIETY WANTED HIM TO BREED BUT IT OFFERED-UP SEX OBJECTS WHO WERE WORRIED ABOUT GETTING PREGNANT ?

Don't they know how GOOD my penis will make them feel?

Don't they know that MEN rule the world?

32

BILL FELT THAT THESE LADIES DIDN'T UNDERSTAND THE MALE LIBIDO ....
ONCE STIMULATED,
IT CANNOT BE TURNED-OFF

THE PRESSURE OF ROILING EJACULATE PUSHES AGAINST A MAN'S LOINS WITH THE MOTIVATION OF A FETUS, DEMANDING BIRTHRIGHT, PUSHING THROUGH THE VAGINA DURING LABOR

THIS FORCE OF NATURE MUST **AND WILL** EXIT THE BODY EITHER BY CONSENTUAL OR FORCED COITUS*

* MASTURBATION IS ANOTHER OPTION BUT ONLY IF THE ALPHA MALE HASN'T BOUGHT THE LADY DINNER

AND THUS BEGAN BILL'S LOVE/HATE RELATIONSHIP WITH THE FEMALE SEX

BILL BEGAN TO BELIEVE THAT
HE WAS IN SOME SORT OF

WAR WITH VAGINAS

HE ASSESED THE ENEMY AND
CAME TO THE CONCLUSION ....

HE COULD AND WOULD WIN
IF HE PRESSED HIS ADVANTAGES
OF
SIZE,
STRENGTH
AND
FINANCIAL PORTFOLIO

35

So, BILL BEGAN TO WEAPONIZE

FIRST ...
HE WORKED OUT
AND MADE HIS
BODY **POWERFUL**

BUT, IN AMERICA,
SINCE <u>MONEY</u> IS MUSCLE .....

HE WENT ALL OUT
TO EARN MONEY &
CONSPICIUOUSLY
CONSUMED THE
TOYS OF WEALTH

HE CRUSHED HIS
COMPETITORS
IN BUSINESS

AND HIRED WOMEN
WHO WOULD SLEEP
WITH HIM

36

AND IF A WOMAN DIDN'T WORSHIP HIS PENIS AFTER ALL OF THAT EFFORT, BILL HAD NO QUALMS ABOUT PUSHING HIS ADVANTAGE TO THE LIMIT ....

"While this scene of bondage is only an example for this book, you DO realize that I control you and could force you to swallow my scrotum?!"

IT WAS WAR AND WOMEN WERE THE ENEMY!

ONE DAY, A WOMAN WHOM BILL HAD **FORCED** TO LOVE HIS PENIS

ACCUSED HIM OF RAPE

BILL PROCLAIMED HIS INNOCENCE !

(and, er ... his "victimhood")

"THIS IS THE FAULT OF SOCIETY," BILL CRIED, "WOMEN ARE BORN TO LOVE MY PENIS"

BUT THE JURY
DIDN'T BUY IT

40

AND NOW, BILL
IS IN PRISON

41

....WHERE BILL IS RETURNED TO THOSE DAYS OF HIS YOUTH WHEN MEN WANTED HIS BODY

MAYBE IT'S WHAT HE WANTED ALL ALONG?

Of COURSE, NOT ALL MEN END UP IN PRISON LIKE BILL ....

THE PERFECT MAN

THOUGH THE LIFE THEY LEAD IS FAR FROM PERFECT AND PERHAPS, FAR FROM THE LIFE THEY WANTED

BILL'S STORY STARTED OUT
WITH A SIMPLE DREAM:
TO HAVE A HAPPY PENIS

BUT DREAMS IN THIS WORLD
ARE FUNGIBLE COMMODITIES

WHATEVER THE REASON OR REASONS OUR
DREAMS BECOME WHAT THEY BECOME ....

WE MEN HAVE THE POTENTIAL TO BE MONSTERS ...

BUT WHEN WE UNDERSTAND THE FORCES
THAT CHALLENGE OUR DEVELOPMENT, WE
HAVE THE POTENTIAL FOR LIVES FREE OF
FRUSTRATIONS THAT CREATE MONSTERS

45

A Final Word

Some men behaving badly make the national headlines. Others behaving badly make the "Police Blotter" of their hometown papers. Still, other men never make it into the papers or the courtroom, but find their lives, and the lives of those they claim to love, devastated by masculinity gone toxic.

Men need to heed the warning. Eighty percent of violent crimes in America are committed by men. Ninety percent of homicides worldwide are perpetrated by men. Each day in the United States there are approximately sixteen thousand reports of domestic violence by men acting out against their partners or spouses.

We men seem to be angry about something. Are we mourning the lost options of our youthful pansexuality? Only we men, each individually, can answer that question. Only we can fix our problem.

What makes a man a man? Courage? Tenderness? Generosity? Confidence? Compassion? It's an open question. But it's abundantly clear what makes a man a dick.

"MEN
CAN
BE
DICKS"

Written and Illustrated by Kichi
©2018 by JAKichi

The End